Allotment Architecture

Allotment
Architecture

PETER HUGHES

REALITY STREET

Published by
REALITY STREET
63 All Saints Street, Hastings, East Sussex TN34 3BN, UK
www.realitystreet.co.uk

First edition 2013

A catalogue record for this book is available from the British Library

ISBN: 978-1-874400-64-6

Acknowledgements

Lynn Deeps and *18* first appeared in publications edited by Mark
Cobley and published by Red Ceilings Press and Knives, Forks &
Spoons Press respectively. *Behoven* was first published by Oystercatcher
Press. *Site Guide* first appeared from The Arthur Shilling Press, edited
by Harry Godwin. Edmund Hardy's Intercapillary Space hosted the
first version of *Berlioz* which is partly collaged from the composer's
memoirs. Some poems also appeared in Cambridge Literary Review,
Ekleksographia, Poetry Wales, Shadow Train, 10th Muse and Tears in
the Fence.

This book is dedicated to my parents, Mary Hughes and the late Cliff
Hughes, who showed me early on how to get off the path in order to
explore, and who continue to support these explorations in different
ways. PETER HUGHES

CONTENTS

LYNN DEEPS

1

I see you board a west-bound bus in clothes
that nearly didn't make it & will not
tire of rubbing you up the right way
just as the seasons look out the window
in the first draft there will probably be
some gravity-related images
but it's best to break through those straight into
heaven sent these moist musical landings
it's a mumbling coalition after
my own heart not to mention the spumy
bowsprit of my voyage round your headland
it looks like we were caught in each other's
headlights & glove boxes for the finest
sentence in the history of transport

2

in the dead of night which is a crap pub
we knew we had to keep driving eastwards
until we reached the end of the country
& then keep going for three albums more
the stars scribbled themselves out of the sky
but in your online planetarium
those perky outlines rearranged the town
around the fragile ash of my roll-up
we sped past dead stacks of Tesco charcoal
dressed in pre-menopausal Northern Light
with a case of western indigestion
& a radio tuned to Belgian funk
in those days we could replenish the tank
without even pulling in off the road

3

it was either porridge boiling over
& jamming another duff microwave
or the next cover version of dance me
to the end of love there's always bacon
& the kind of impermeable gear
we need to face the sun's excesses
we must have walked that dog five thousand miles
before its legs wore right down to its name
but none of us lost that first startled look
you physically need to get into space
cadetship in that casual freelance sphere
we selected instead of worm banking
whatever the hour you were always there
to rub out the edges of our bodies

4

as further uncontrollable urges
whistle the north in sideways down the wash
to lift the top right off our potting shed
my mind returns to times that never were
like you in one of those swerving surges
in a day-glo & pneumatic lifeboat
your hand clutching the important hard bit
we used to grill collateral for lunch
steadfast in our hatred of butterflies
& their selfish brassica ravishes
the siren always took us by surprise
& is blu-tacked to the back of my mind
whose singed walls still echo with the first time
I ever explored your fishing village

5

of course some said at this stage of the game
is it wise to dive through the boundary
just buy some head-socks & take a picnic
along to a Joanna Newson gig
we cut the grass & think she may have done
I've got a brand new pair of rollerskates
& I left my heart in Newport Pagnell
but in the end we chose to escape through
a tunnel & thence by microlite to
sparsely populated regions such as
the old days eventually grew out of
we consulted the Fakenham birdbath
bulging ice lens still ignoring twilight
yet galvanising our faces in moon

6

the rogue gnocchi of Abergavenny
pursued us through cold nights of restless sleep
& later formed a cash-in-hand band for
weddings or birthdays & passing yours SATs
the only real security was speed
but with the second-hand Fiesta hitched
to a home-made marine-ply caravan
we couldn't underestimate the risks
the alcoholic SAS man swore
if we kept on the move around Norfolk
we would confuse everyone including
ourselves & that is certainly working
imagining the place where we started
we still don't know penguins have solid bones

7

judging from my own depreciation
& my year's not even in the guidebook
or the fact my tongue won't last till Sunday
I reluctantly acknowledge at least
intellectually that we may not last
eternally in the hairy bone sense
new subatomic & cosmic wonders
will not be able to catch us ducking
the construction of more local branches
of Asda than Wisbech where we bought this
perspex eyewash dish of chicken liver
simple at the back of the freezer cheap
& overlooked wearing a tight-fitting
balaclava of rime outlive us too

8

this may have been you smiling in the dark
& that may have been your left stocking top
the asymmetry of the saxophone
I don't think you can call that a salad
although up to your elbows in growbag
you & the fire whisper sensible routes
through a complete history of power cuts
you even got me up on the dance floor
along with the tips of your fingers & things
in umber pubs smelling of cigarettes
& the small faces turned up in the night
to the gentle Wicklow rain for instance
through the fragility of eastern night
you make the light last longer on the water

9

daddy was a rafter in a coal mine
mummy deconstructed cardboard boxes
out behind the Co-op on weekday nights
with some help from the other immigrants
it was tricky to focus on weeding
the kitchen with you in your nomad shorts
& modified onion-chopping snorkel
yet still we made our way through the cliches
of sentence construction & assumption
by planting conkers in window boxes
then trundling down the aisle at 3 a.m.
towards the waiting pilchards & shampoo
yes love was always in the air but that
wasn't usually where we wanted it

10

though it's true that we won't last for ever
tonight we ought to put the dustbin out
things have a habit of lasting longer
than the daily mail says they're going to
I woke up this morning & it was still
the night before I tried to go to bed
a grope of hunger drifts in on the breeze
from the chip-shop which closed six hours ago
you don't need a tardis to fuck with time
it's best to jig along its back with love
until the caravan tips right over
that's why we don't plug it in to the grid
we just set light to stuff in handy fields
usually starting with each other

BEHOVEN

1

we suddenly lost interest
in such impossible pasts
lifting our heads towards
the river elsewhere
a new jetty stood beside
the old beyond repair
time mends an idea
slips its moorings
swings out into the current
& a kneeling figure
works on
pausing only to reach
for three more nails
& place them gently
between her lips

2

hello
cuckoo drunk I
come through hedges
sideways in September twigs
flick back & whip you
in a list of
reasons to be cheerful
with asterisks

3

        screw up page & wipe stars
       appear & tighten
      screws on loft-ladder
       tip-toe between Bo
        Diddley & a Renoir lavender
         ribbons in a mass of red
               hair run for the bus
          bed pushed to the window
        head sticking out into the sky
             a cantilevered plank
          relieves neck muscles
vans brought morning in the rain
however many nights the head
stayed out the rent remained
     the same fuel bills rose & turned red
          skip to the loo
        & sing a ring
          of shaving cream
               & rust   no credit

4

when the aerial stops oscillating
you clearly hear the sweeping
up of broken plates
hail Maria ave Harold
another raindrop starts trickling
down the pane then sets off
sideways at extraordinary speed
to reach the frame
& kick back up into the sky

wolf cubs skip into a gale warning

we trundle diagonally downhill
on an asymmetric sledge
towards the least attractive stretch
of tree-line a cough & a jump
each path leads down as well as up
but there's only one way to go
if you want bread
oh & bring it back

5

scurry up the dune to supply
lines hindered by each finger
showing off to the next
bat around the head
this butterfly in a dark shed

would you play it the same way twice

after forgotten atrocities
visionary themes go
up & down in a lift
growing medium
ideas cancel each other out
gravity & hiccoughs
mimes of paranoia
twitching through the forest of itself
poised & well-hung
the magic cherries
turn out to be
peaches

6

the song's high fitful
clarity surfs churning
low-pressure systems
relentless on-shore winds
& a new moon calling
water home to nowhere
                    seething tidal races
unnavigable gestures under glass
            & as the ink dries it fades
like a note   as in note
        in the canopy live birds
who've never seen the ground
or heard of darkness falling
fathoms below through
        cracked notions
trunks & hourly precipice
sooty mould dusts knuckles
in the ministry of growth
on the path behind the wood
a dusty nut
    splits & roots
    in the grey
        swaying rucksack

rain on tiny wooden
wheelbarrows & tramp steamers
rabbits wash their ears behind
 the hill where we make it up
  these pretty trills transport
    soil beyond the national
          borders the rabbit is dropsy
               flicks back into the guts
                    of the earth
          some died or moved away
               after summer fetes
                   when strangers
          with sledge-hammers
          & shorts passed
          the whole piano
      through a bangle

8

tomorrow fell from the sky
with bits of food in the corners
lenses rinsed in leaking
vats of rough red wine
any behaviour was being
philosophical was my impression
of a bird being attacked by another
bird before they both sat quietly
in a tree
becoming beautiful is often
the rhythm of concern
rocking to & fro
before the knock on the door
with time & a mouthful of nails
research shows
the fate of each remnant
to be more interesting
than the fate of the bulk
of each roll

9

bring bonny back
to the dockside
freed by waiting
for a morning
of details
tight trainers
coffee containing pale grit
a three-legged dog loping
past grinning into the wind
& the Copenhagen boat
tending left
but several hands
push it north-east
to more frosty stacks
of Baltic timber
& potential passengers
with indecision & fists
stuffed in mufflers
there is comfort in the story
sung without words
a sunlit liquid shiver
again we turned & tried
remembering things
we'd never known

10

swept down natural steps
to the pool at the bottom
of the mountain
water & other phenomena
restlessly quest after
lunch & in June
there was a lull
where sweet English waters
rose through chalk beds
to dance through dips
& cushions in the surface
of the pool in dappled
alder shade
this freshwater spring
& water boatmen

the scrumping went
according to plan

brassicas netted
there's nowhere to roost
if you're a cabbage
white butterfly

11

impossible to creep up
on the shelf from behind
take your time eastwards
in stomach-churning calm

it's no good walking past like that
even if it is called a patio

lethargic topiary
up beyond the mitten
the face in space
all chapped lips
autumn stars

12

apricots & black
coffee by the mattress
on the floorboards we breathed
an aftershock of happiness

cotton refuge

glide between wing-beats

your memories coming up the stairs

O Vienna!

13

nocturnal reconnaissance

bring your own weather

shacks of the deep south
stacked with empty casks
& the last seven words
from the crossroads

the flag factory has closed
& crowds move down
towards the docks
waving wooden spoons

14

a high-tide line
  of dead ladybirds
    in a world without sound

      pulse in a crevice

    & words sail
into altered time of dark
 red wine for several
    hours now years & geese
      migrating over
            the house

15

an element of shanty
far inland
 is irresistible
    now whistled
            now hummed
          we are night
locked inside factories
     that pickle fish
          in Bonn

16

he would stalk
  the winter quarters
    of the circus
  glaring at the bears

17

                grave & shimmering
            restlessness this wasn't
              what they meant by
                salami keeping
                out the cold
        intensities of autumn light
        illuminate years
        of reckless calm
          the ballroom now a surgery
            like a prayer in the night
              the poetry soars way up
    towards the very edges
      of the imagination
            almost reaching
                the hair-line

18

sound check feel your way in
before the hall fills up
saw a house martin click by
saw an inch from the back leg
of the piano for the entry
of the milliner's cousin Allegra
feather bobbing to the loo
in black   deft as in canary
divertimento road works

over the hill with a sapling
protruding from the top of the knapsack

the fact that the song's
without words
allows one to continue

clock tock   glass inflamed
thin bell pings & sears
the mind's four
fissured towers

19

miserable simplicities
recline under the fingers
whispering September
plane leaves along the banks
of the Seine cannot be heard
from here unlike the fight
across the street
& the piano lesson
that neither teacher
nor student attend

20

as the territorial
army fanfare
fades in western breeze

a cadet hitches home

it wasn't what
I thought
he said
we do

21

they joined hands
        to form a lake
  in which nothing could live

    strands & coagulations
of night snagged
 inside the sinuses
   lungs & vaults as
            the years pass

        oranges
blue with fame

22

yank the box
        wide open
                rupturing the hinges

rearrange kindling

    do daily matter numerously
open imaginary box
    with deftness & delicacy
      lift the hopes of stranger
        neighbours getting into
            fervid teems

23

dusk twigs tighten
slip & whip the skin
in front of the face
rock flour & chippings
dragging the feet back
from under the body
down the scree slopes
of the system
some dust
probably settles
on the surface
of the river
tomorrow

irreversible panic
softly peeps through
the skin split
migrate

24

& I saw her standing there
            an unrepeatable moment
followed by another
            manual triplet
        left in the air
to negotiate with England
waves around its legs
& that is how she stood
  in the sky at the end
    of the pier
      thy pink &
        smouldering
              alto

25

I didn't even know we had a
trampoline   *trampoline*
the view from the neighbours
  so diverse *alla*
   tedesca plus mat &
    cuckoo

    the songs
   of this estate
   are beautifully
     mistaken

it is worse to be nationalistic
in the bass
  between the moments
   when the French invade
    & when they leave
     ease each other up
      from fetid nests

26

transformations of farewell
revolved & swallowed
  I would keep you near by
     breathing
       pace the restless second
  question far
            into the night
insomnia in C minor
rawness through the throat
eyes & pronouns
       freedom with bells on
             growing into
         nights full of lights
        that dance along
      imaginary alleys
     opening onto
    renovated streets

27

I think therefore I hover
 hot & cold earth
  live & neutral turning into
   new dreams of Bach
      membrane
          ruptured
unity & resolution changed
        nothing about this
just another person in the world
          drinking coffee
    I think of happiness
             sleeping
   on the banks
   of inner streams
all our voices making up
        for lost time
     with lost time

28

sung across the loch
forever lost in Europe
remembering the cello
forgotten in a foreign
landlord's loft
some melodies are endless
the edges disappearing
in a mist that gently rises
over insight & perspective
trousers ready for the wash
determination to march on
senseless by learning the key
routes & striding blind
to the dimly-lit waterside bar
& a short-cut home underwater
nobody there
in the changing spaces between
moonlight shadows your own
tentative steps towards
the tether's end
a compartment
larger than the whole night sky
where this one love once lived
& yodelled across the cold
car-park in bare feet

29

if you bang your head hard
enough on a hard enough
wall blood will trickle down
  & complicate your trousers
    still further futurity calls

            correction fluid

            some nights are more
              of a trip than others
        huge wood & ivory wreckage in gulfs
of red wine its tidal races break another
bottle on the bows of the self & trundle
down the slipway into dumb buoyancy
    a tribute to the laws of physics
    & philosophy of listening
      as the cure chews your head off
            the spaces either side
            are symbolising nails & rain
it was good to have an idea of what it could do
even if what it could do was dance on the pyre
            of its own conception until the fuel
          was spent & history smouldered
              in the blackened ruins
              of the organ

30

the length of the phrase extends
to include every other
 the bass remains a stranger
  as do all the other voices
   in the choir of day
    which sings night home
      for rest &
                  decomposition
                    each figure
            follows the other
       over the horizon

31

    an uplift of daylit
     singing suspends
    the temporary sky
  in gaps between these folk
songs of the dispossessed
 we watched when bread
was cast upon the waters
     & eaten by ducks
     the winter afternoon
     smells again of
      homelessness
     thus small waves fall
    along the edges
   deep seas of weariness
  pale flame burns unseen
in pale afternoons of sunlight
a bell tolls at low tide
  with unexpected modulations
   of tomorrow   not so much
     her words as her tone
     & a feeling that the sky
      awakes from hibernation
     while water surreptitiously
     frees the hull from soft
      sands of sense
        & knowledge

32

a sense of pit-props giving
   way below the head galleries
      collapse & open into
       smoking moonlit gullies
       earthquake flutters
   paddle in dark water

      here where words
          were stars
            loom

SITE GUIDE

for Heine, and the Caravan Club

site 1

roll up for the paragliding donkeys
or synchronised three-legged dogging
but first   perform a one-man mexican wave
to yawn   greet dawn   appease the demons
in the clifftop maze   which points to itself
eventually   the floor of the caravan dries
then we heave the whole box
clockwise 35 degrees
to follow the sun   & so on
if what we know is wrong
suspended in a sea of ignorance & cack
(leave space) suggest-abilities raise seal heads
submerge again without apparently inhaling
shopping results for the tibetan book of the dead
your cart is currently empty
it has become necessary to imagine
these companions & their fleeting theme tunes
this one blending
tallis & the shithouse lilies
is norman wisdom dead yet
if not   why not
head circus parade talk to me until
sometimes I stand so still
the rats come out to wash in peace

site 2

       golf within 10 miles but safer to read
    the small henderson room
  for medicinal purposes
  whose ash & goats are these
   on the far side of the blackthorn
     three hyacinths (intensely blue)
    do what all the flowers do by night
  there are lots of little fliers in the toilet
       advertising free delivery
       of meals to throw at trees
    & worlds of fake attraction
    let's go to vaulted vacancy
where the psychic octopus circles overhead
     on a festo airpenguin
   then again the keltic seal-juggler
  sounds exactly what we need
 after wrestling with decision
& a vietnamese river cobbler
to the accompaniment of cornish rap
& the region's characteristic ronsealed mdf lutes
   the state of the evening decays
       to squatting on rock
  as the final tin of old speckled
   hen turns immensely dark

site 3

the moon's inexplicably abandoned
in a different night of strangers
devoid of pewter or cinnamon tunes
or those of hawthorn   straw   or fennel
larkspur / curlew
she said when I end this line
I'll count to three & you'll awake
forget this ever happened   1   2
you can smell tcp
for up to three weeks after you die
we opted for an hour or two of music
luigi tenco megamix
a bit of dr loco
a transfer deal involving
several pet shop boys
with a neighbour's plastic suitcase
she left in the rain before dawn
in her I fucked leonard cohen t-shirt
the wrong registration number
etched on the caravan window
there is nothing in the field
except this empty grapefruit half
two slugs nestling in the
brilliantly white soft bottom

site 4

those who danced were thought insane
by those who couldn't hear the music
according to the old nietzsche hit
yet this is where they all relax
divertimento macchiato
o spirits of the airwaves
batter my heart & wrap it in tabloid
paper-mache pig banks
daubed with tar
so many sloping pitches
wedges & ice-picks are strongly recommended
beautiful indian hair may be bought
at the harbour of chamfered-toot-saints
where prawns nibble dead skin
from the feet of rich pink men
who make decisions on water
boarding & commission
in mature gardens
deep in quiet light
under the fine star fields around altair
in aquila
mrs hales as euphrosyne
helps discord
& the winds fall into haven

site 5

    shit-cake ponies back into awnings
we line up for the contest:
 who looks
   most like a cross
      between paolo nutini
           & a hillman imp
             that summer of donovan pâté
             logo by creeley
 I knew my swollen loaf
how true & yet how now
  brown horse is never now enough
    don't leave without trying a molecatcher's pie
               & paying for it   through dappled
                   afternoons of otter racing
              rippled with despair & sobriety
      in peak season the whole park hums
                 with unwashed kids
              dyspraxic lego professionals
            the whiff of snagged crab
   turn up in february & celebrate with
      accommodating locals who put
         slug pellets right around
        the border of the county
      come valentine's day

site 6

it only takes a moment
to find a space
disconnect
stare out of the window
welcome home
get used to living
without a coherent world view
in a temporary house
called *wet paint*
a building made entirely out of doors
allotment architecture is
the region's source of civic pride
deconstructed palettes
irregular lengths of unplaned timber
openings hinged with strips of bald tyre
swallow the sun with the sea
as you swim through
the edges of the world
it moves up & down
three millimetres
on your neck   & tickles
your body turning blue
before being
mounted on wheels again

site 7

sounds of an offstage skeleton stomp
sung by a delicate province
kindle the senses with light (as if
one person's voice contained this brass
avoid nattering at launches
or sportsday result mix-ups
veni creator spiritus
in two years' time it'll all sound normal
who has the strength
to break the bonds of desire
who has three legs
who has the paracetamol
what cannot be described
is here accomplished
the eternally feminine driving us onward
but stopping for a top-up at the butcher's
you interact & then withdraw
you interact & then withdraw & wait
evaporation poaches little rock pools
to shimmering new substance
with insufficient fruit to ferment
they thought the oil was natural
that lightning would ignite it
& any christening kills a lot of birds on legs & fish

site 8

bring your antiquated tackle
link with catatonic starers here
where there is where we stare
for fear of having no feet left
the warden is authorised to tasar
autistic recipients of fuck-all
to remind them saturday night fever
never really died but twitches
looks a lot like living every month
with very little kit just iceland
flat-pack crem fuel with added
laxative & this white dust
don't miss the august homophobic spree
turn right again after the miniature
pony centre you can't miss it
tucked between the hedgehog hospice
& the styptic pencil factory
tv poor
ideal for your mature splendour
collapsing in a puddle
mushroom whittling within ten metres
I am the bud
on an imaginary tree
no you're not dave

site 9

sat nav not recommended & all
distances in leagues & pounds
the rejigged atrocity theme park
is just a tram-ride & rally
away from your himalayan flume
plastic ditch experience
bring your own cash & intelligence
restrictions apply tv still poor
try your hand at donkey feeding
with a lapful of padding
from the top of the topless bus
glimpse some of the largest
houses in the universe
round off the day with profound
frustration & a sharp barney
or relax in one of our locals
who rarely throw darts
at your legs on purpose
some of our visitors come
back especially those
who drove off without
reconnecting their caravans
some of us have nothing
to attach it to love

site 10

while some may enjoy dorking
golfers will certainly
relish swinging through landscaped
cells in this surprisingly untouristy
area of kidderminster
where the dinosaur
park just about sums it up
hardy walkers embrace
the chance of going out for
cigarettes & the park boasts
although this site has no toilet
guests like tanks & monkey
world sometimes glimpsing
a hunter's moon or fat controller
the jigsaw museum is second to
a network of poachers' culverts
used as recently as next tuesday
the sullen attractions of france
gateway to the east
are just a short cycle-ride
away from france
several times a season
sunsets are recognisable as such
from your own revised pavilion

site 11

put the sparkle back into your privacy cubicle
with a durable sojourn in one of the south's
   most northerly excuses & compliments
         twang your awning peg
      nestled where the sun rarely sets
        or indeed rises you will savour
   factory shopping outlets you'd forgotten
      & get back in touch with your own dutch quarter
               where traffic noise can be expected
                  enjoy the local cycle-path or goat
               before numbing your remaining senses
                  with a tasty german import
         & glimpses of the region's frozen laundry
            sculptures in the awesome precincts
                  of where to choose a sofa
            the legendary dwarfs' causeway
               & the angel of the north
               are just a short flight from
   the end of your optimistic suspension
   of disbelief as a twenty-pound deposit
   is required for the electronic barrier
      guided vegetable preparation may be
      available depending on season & staff
         disciplinary procedure outcomes

site 12

                        although tents & caravans are still banned
                    this site boasts six taps & a lawn
                as well as much fresh air several excellent
            hedges with local attractions & swindon to hand
            five-aside football cricket rounders swimming
                boules badminton cycling pogoing
                    skating surfing & yoga are also discouraged
                        so explore the sites of numerous battles
                    throughout its fine estates
                in the car-park of aldi & its predecessor
                the visitor centre is mainly closed
                but this won't affect your enjoyment
            of the recycling facilities adjacent to
        a perfect english village which is
    out of bounds to tourists though postcards
repackaged sandwich pickle & guides
    to imaginary ufos are all popular
        in the sense of existing   no arrivals
                        before three or after four are necessary
                            further afield the retired volcano
                    now flattened is almost irresistible
                    the fairytale city of cambridge
                & a visit to king's college
                    chapel is a musty

site 13

a quaint & inward-looking venue
harks back to pre-enclosure sheep
& is within easy reach of a takeaway
outlet amongst others special fees
apply to all those little extras such as
pup tents   mats   hair-dos
& temporary erections
no showers for the disabled but
average rainfall is high so
families often organise a one-night
stop *en route* to the continent
calls may be monitored & doctored
for the purposes of fraud & recreation
listen out for duck
& oasthouse ghosts
wolves wild boar & estate workers
often stow away for chunnel fun
the miniature railway skirts bleak
house & monkey world
which in retrospect
spoils more archaeological remains
than most visitors find time for
beach within 45 miles as it's
44 miles away tv poor

site 14

the 19th century has just left
on a tractor without tyres
so that's two world wars coming up
don't forget the famous illuminations
as we haven't got any
care required at the mini-roundabout
& crater near the entrance try
toddler pit & unlicensed bar
shotgun shooting limited access
when speedway or dog racing on
countless traditional seaside attractions
like paddling are just a train
ride away as are the local broads
withheld numbers ignored
tv poor but radio works quietly
loose dogs shot
drugs available after hours at
adjacent rspb hide plus
strumpet den experience by
arrangement (exc thus) & hop
like a prince festival with
local truffle-hunting action
& indoor pond-dipping
[cash only]

site 15

~~a tunnel to hell plunges through each pitch~~
see the woodland adventure log
as featured on songs of praise bloopers
or be a tudor rampart for tide stemming
synchronised midges & the ever
popular hive of activity according
to the press a haven for the over
50s active types & men
drop in to the Margaret Thatcher dolls
hospital & badger sanctuary
or watch out for the wildlife
bbq display team for the riskiest
hoop-la in the north
some aircraft noise & light gunfire
is to be expected by brass-rubbers
of all ages   Henley is up a road
traditionalists from all walks of life
will relish the narrow range of
cultural references visible here
you are probably well placed
to visit cadbury world
lovers of real ale should go
to the supermarket & oak
where legend has it

18

1

fairest
it is time
to fly like an eagle
you might
want to take
your boots off first

2

again we bit
into the insides
of our own mouths
remoulding the horizon
squeak
home on the range

3

run tongue over
scar tissue
another year has passed
in which no one
has employed
the inflatable canoe

4

the last place
to look
for mosquitoes
is in the dark
& inaccessible hollows
of your own flute

5

& this is where
the new nationalists
shaved her head
& left four tufts
in place of children

6

fábrica de luz
& yet another haunted gulley
the sun continues
to die
increasingly
distracting
don't you think

7

we laddered two more pairs
of harem pants
whilst escaping
back into the wild
electric
& accommodating hills

8

on the outskirts of the capital
contemporary machines
continue to slice sand
stone for the old
prestigious projects

9

Dave Shrimp says
the big society
will be surrounded
by fires of bald tyres
& borders of yew

10

while Fred Chopin
lifts the hem
of another widow's frock
sleet types two
more pages on the window

11

in a history of Norfolk
flamenco volume eleven
we sense mucus
turn to lemon juice
speech to brine

12

mosquitoes infiltrate
the writer & the written
a black dog paws the moon
still flinching in shallow water

13

two great display stacks
fall inwards as you enter
the supermarket sideways
in bed
hurtling after more cheese

14

& your fingernails
became the shells
of empty mussels
tendons reaching back into depths
for salt & rim

15

they are eating
boots of softest leather
when you mow mushrooms
they say in deep
serious voices
woffle

16

leaves fall
on these two ragged mats
left out to dry
by the dead
couple
their patterns
inseparable

17

for £230 you could be
a fine Spanish fungus
on Andrew Motion's table
then secretly lubricate hymn too

18

you will take tiny walks
in a tiny garden
damsons & mint
the stars of autumn slowly reappear

BERLIOZ

Part 1

1

first you're sat
on your dad's lap
then your face
is grey as the grave

you've used up
the years
you waited for
in a cold wind

cold as the winter
of your birth

you look around seeing nothing
but second nature

mountains to south & east
more geomorphology
to north & west

the long deluge of silt
precipitating through your body

2

my eldest sister & I
took first communion
at the convent

we left at six in the sacred
spring morning trembling
with family irritation
in poplar leaves & fingers
anticipation a speechless host

young women in white

the crass priest
called me first
as I was male

but a deeper music
had swung in
around & through me

all lacewinged

mystical &

           glandular

3

our father
now a compôt
of All-Bran & opium

his stomach
eating itself for years

a long sandbank accumulating
along the west bank

strapped me to my schooling

I clenched my eyes
& sailed through the lids
to Palestine
then southern seas

every baguette
bought from a souk

I skimmed the Arabian Sea
was hymned by the Mouths of the Ganges
glided through the islands & straits
of Borneo & Java

Sumatra affected my breathing

4

he perspired blood
to teach me Latin

I sailed the South China Seas
in my chair
oblivious to learning objectives

or was paralysed
by licks of magic:

she searched
for heaven's light
& groaned when
then it found her

overwhelmed me
capsizing in A minor

yet when I was
overcome
with emotion
it was he who pretended
to be too tired to go on

such grace

such embarrassed grace
our father

5

I mainlined on music

& I mainlined on love

I tripped on genetically modified lines
in the white house among the vines

they tell me there are holidays each year

Estelle & her little pink boots
still wring me out

she was eighteen & I was twelve
but part of my heart is still on her shelf

o she knew
& once she asked me to dance with her
in front of the world

I managed to spin
right through the surface of France

one day I'll tell you
about the cave paintings I made

6

my father
fed up with
din on the whistle
taught me to play it
then bought me a flute

& then all the bourgeois shenanigans -
reading music
theory   song
ensemble

                    harmony & pain
                    guitar in the dark

writing songs to her elbows & vines

her hair & high air

her feet:

what good is a world
of guitars & flutes
if I can't have you
in your little pink boots?

7

you will be a doctor   he said

I will be a Gluck   a Haydn

my hair said standing up to be counted

I have seen my first full score

now I know what it is
to spit a mouthful of Fitou
against my hand on the cavern wall
& feel the shape of my soul
cohere out of sight
as my body gently turns
into the dust

8

in the revolution

I went for a walk in England
where many poets bicker
between hedges & libraries

but now I'm back & fiercely indignant
music lessons have been disrupted
in the most intolerable manner

what is one to do
except talk about oneself ?

9

& so to Paris to study medicine

Alphonse took me to the cutting
rooms in the Hospice de la Pitié

the floor a spongy bed of human off-cuts

small birds scrapping
for beakfuls of lung
rats sampling fragments
of damp backbone

hacked-open heads invited me
to a private view of my future

I was out through the open window
& off up that road
before you could say
Jacques Robinson

Part 2

1

but I had to go back
to the cutting room floor
I rasped   sawed   inhaled decay
                slipped on innards

donated the root of an angel's wing
to a famished rat with
the evacuated eyes of a critic

but then   the Opéra

it was like moving
from rowing boats in the park

to the decks of majestic three-masters
riding all the distant inner oceans

suddenly it was music to
the power of itself

it was cosmic
imagining & writing

unimaginable numbers

2

forcing the hacksaw
through a stranger's cranium
the next day
I hummed a tune
conducting with my eyebrows

the kindly gifts of destiny

I practically ran back to the opera
& was chromatically damaged
by a cor anglais   crying
the hymn that floated
        my first communion

then I found
the Conservatoire library
was open to the public

the manuscripts of
Gluck treasure
like Shakespeare's notes

once my eyes & ears had played Gluck
all pretence of medicine
was rinsed down the sink

& I held up the triumphant hand
of an artist

alone like Lear
in the quiet & failing light

3

when convinced
I wouldn't give
up writing
in the name of
all that's holy
my Catholic
mother cursed me

back in Paris
I survived
on private lessons
prune & raison sandwiches
& an inexhaustable
wealth of tone & light
flowing into
poetry & water

I lost weight
& composed myself
with luxurious
orchestrations
desperate pulses
rippling in & out
spreading well upstream
& downriver

don't confuse art
with camouflaging yourself
in landscape

that happens later
up the crem
down the pit

4

below a certain temperature
there can be no reaction

one night as I
conducted clouds

the sky kicked & split
earthing through me

making me brilliant &
dumb with shock

Harriet Smithson
was Ophelia then Juliet

was Shakespeare writing
much of my future

she singed & sang my surfaces
stewed my innerness

every molecule touched by
irreversible change

sleep escaped from
strange nocturnal presence

tracking me across the
room & world

another chorus of feelings

5

I trod the Paris streets
like time

& through the madness
I can count the bouts of sleep

on the fingers
of her left hand

- collapsed in a dark field of corn
  on the edge of the city

- worn out in any meadow
  under autumn sun

- burrowed in snow banked up
  on the banks of the Seine

- with my head on the table
  between my own knife & fork
  in the Café du Cardinal

not reassuring the waiters

6

& that sudden
multiplication
of dark matter
within transformed
for ever the gravities
& orbits of my
life I wrote back
to Shakespeare
& I wrote back to her
the configuration
of my inner river
& the devastated
landscape of my
floating heart
after the flood

leave it out on Tuesdays

7

the whole world

the empty bed

your absent river

8

I practically dragged
Lesueur to
Beethoven's 5th

he was so scared
of giving an opinion

Christ he was
so moved &
disconcerted
that at the end
he went to put
        his hat on
& couldn't find
his head

9

worshipping Harriet
from afar
I didn't notice
Camille breathing
next to me
teaching piano
piano as I
taught guitar
to shadows

Part 3

1

so gifted so
what is that
it's not just
Camille though
there's Mme Moke
moanin' mini
the mother
whose forearms
are forewarned

2

she wants to
know exactly how
her baguette
will be buttered

sister Nanci
what you said
about our
fortune being
founded only
on our talents
worried her a lot

straightening doilies
till they tear

3

Camille Camille
I love the dark
hair of her
looking through
her blue sky eyes
at who the
hell am I
      when she told me
she loved me
my ears blinked
& stuttered

4

I had to win
the Institute prize
for money status
& the gong
I resisted
each temptation
to compose
a Berlioz

I gave them
what they wanted
as the sounds
& vibrations of
revolution turned
streets & facades
to intimate whispers
my redeeming
percussion &
Promised Land
Camille & sound

5

for three glorious days
the people were sublime

I even heard them singing
Berlioz in the street
                my War Song

I went to join in
without letting on
& over ambitiously
tried to right the tempo
as the crowd grew
& the times changed

we could hardly move

three National Guardsmen
kept audience & choir apart
& even passed around
their caps in a whip-round
for those injured
in the uprising

people coughed up
as much for the absurdity
as for the victims

we reversed like dogs
guided by sheep

& backed into the
Galerie Colbert
hemmed in & squeezed
to sing again
from the upstairs window
of a haberdasher's shop

what else but the Marseillaise?

6

everyone stood nicely
shut up & listened

as we held forth
like the bloody Pope

circumambient silence
verse after verse after verse

until I shouted SING

& damn me if they
didn't all start singing
simultaneously
in that confined space

a perfect performance
unscripted & refined

full of ragged passion
like the voice of France

for a moment I passed
out on that wave

I won the Prix de Rome
& scuttled around
the Institute with the biggest
hair in Europe

7

when the Symphonie fantastique
was performed even moaning
Mini Moke was impressed

we are to marry
Camille & I
when I return from Rome

in the morning
I leave for the south

my parents' house
& then the Alps

I have the Prix de Rome
& thus am exiled for months

away from the sites of my art
& heart

it's not the right time
it goes without saying
there is no such thing

8

I couldn't face the mid-winter Alps
so I headed for the port of Marseilles

I've seen cosier graveyards
in the rankest armpits of Paris

than the stinking sties that bobbed there
moored inside the biggest piss-pot in the world

after days steering clear of the worst
wrecks stenches & villains I bumped into

some *simpatici* Italians bound for
Livorno on a Sardinian brig

we had to feed & fend for ourselves
throughout the 4 day journey

so we stocked up for a week
& eased out onto the glittering sea

the Mediterranean miracle
& lunch in the salt & vinegar air

mixing Italian accents with French wine
our stories & songs became richer
strangers by the hour

9

in fact all the other passengers
were Italian

one claimed
to have captained
Byron's boat
down the coast of Italy
to Greece

I loved his
descriptions of gold-braid
alcohol & orgies
too much to demur

seven years now
since the great man died
it feels like none

Part 4

1

I suppose
someone must have been
Byron's skipper

at one point
Byron asked him below
in the turmoil
of another storm
for a game of cards

as the sea   storm & night
got further out of hand

everything & everyone
went everywhere

Byron staggered
back to the table
before anyone else
had worked out
where they were

he gestured to our
farouche captain
to reshuffle & deal

con piacere signore
growled the dogged Venetian

eliciting a wink
& a punch on the arm
he can still feel
from Childe Harolde

2

as night fell &
sky thickened
around our tilting
fairground shed
I saw every gilded stitch
& satin panel on
the sailor's faded
clothes which suddenly
became the absence
of all ambition
fetid groping
raddled posturing
glowing myth

I'd already sailed
away with ghosts

Shelley washed up

9$^{1}/_{2}$ stone of crab bait

we'll go no more a floating

we got no nearer Leghorn
the currents of the night
undid the western evening breezes
we stayed in sight of Nice
for three whole days
until a terrifying Alpine northerly
plunged into the ship
& all its rigging shuddered
the captain ordered too much sail
which dragged us drenched & shaken

at an unholy angle to the choking
waves
                    but Italy bound

3

churning into the Gulf of Spezia
at midnight the storm
impossibly worsened &
tried to tear us from the world

Byron's skipper gripped a soaking rail
& swore through his teeth at this
suicidal captain slapped against the helm
& fifteen sails still set in the black
imploding heart of the tempest

suddenly a great gust stamped on the ship
& nearly plunged her under
our hearts & tongues capsized
as the captain sprawled & flailed
under stampeding herds of barrels

at that moment Byron's skipper
grabbed the wheel himself
ordering the crew through the storm
to stop pestering God & the Madonna
take in the screaming sails & release
the throbbing tensions from the ship
which straight away stood up & eased
the barging winds out through its rigging

so we dragged into Livorno harbour
like a dog with a broken back leg
a mad wind still singing through one snotty sail

we stowed ourselves in the Black Eagle inn
wet & cumbersome luggage dead weight

passport control   Villa Medici   Cafe Greco
put them in order of vacant squalor
as your starter for ten

4

when in Rome
why not do as I did
pace fret & moan
& go to Florence
to wait for the French post

yet when it finally arrived
it fisted a cheap corkscrew
into my heart
Madame Moke announces
the engagement of Camille
to Mr Pleyel
the toxic French ink swam in my eyes
with Florentine light

ah the mad Renaissance clarity

I would kill them all
then end it all
& drain the mucky lake for good

5

my intention gift-wrapped
I plunged into the French milliners
overlooking the steady
flow of the Arno
& in front of the owner's expressionless eyes
began some serious post-revolutionary
retail therapy

she promised faithfully
that by the time the mail coach
left for France at 6 o'clock
I would have my dress
my hat & veil in deep green
a maid's outfit to be proud of

I recrossed the unaffected Arno
in a fit of personal climate change
en route to the Hotel des Quatre Nations
& completed my deranged free-range
arrangements noting on the score
of the Ball Scene from the Symphonie fantastique
unfinished

6

if you perform it in my absence
just double the flute passage
with clarinets & horns an octave lower
when the theme returns for the last time

then let the full orchestra
have the final chords
as at least some kind of ending

I closed the annotated score
packed a few clothes
loaded two double-barrelled pistols
& packed my little bottles
of laudanum & strychnine
then wandered twitching
through the gorgeous Tuscan afternoon
like a cocky dog with rabies

7

at 5 o'clock I went back to the shop
to try on the frock
what a perfect fit
you can't beat the French
for hang & cut

the till girl tried to tell me
I'd overpaid
the owner
quickly stuffed the extra notes
into the drawer
& was very sincere

ah sir you are charm itself
your performance
will bring the house down

8

I caught the coach
& swayed northwards in silence
my mouth stone-dry & closed

the coachman had sensibly
unloaded & hidden my pistols
in case we were attacked

but as we entered Genoa
the urchins fishing with
chicken-foot bait
& pungent urban folksong
the awful realisation docked
at the weathered wall of my consciousness:
I'd lost my disguise
                    we'd changed coaches
at Pietra Santa & my avenging angel kit
was still stowed aboard the first carriage

9

more shopping
in the first four dress shops
they threw up their hands
at the monstrous demand:
an appropriate ensemble
in less than six hours
in green
sir you joke
but the fifth nodded sagely
& mobilised a crack platoon
of Ligurian seamstresses
again
game on

Part 5

1

the border police
& over-excited immigration officers
in their new uniforms
egged on by the gutter press
had meanwhile hatched the notion
that I was sneaking back & forth
between commie France
& regal Italy
in order to foment revolution
it was time to move on
& in spite of my high-tech hardware
& green comfy software
the currents of life & art began to
dissolve the grains of hatred
lodged between my teeth

2

I can't say when my daring plan
softened to old ideas
but I know that for a magic month
I wandered in & out of Nice
through air full of its own music
I watched the sea from orange groves
& vines of sunlit hills for days
that grew inside me like leaves
alone I wrote as naturally
as a shoal turns in the tide
& I turned towards Rome

3

after enduring gang-show opera
down through the peninsula
I arrived in Rome in time
for the feast of Corpus Christi
what treats were now in store
what heavenly aesthetics
a circus trundling into town
would have breathed more spirituality
than this confectionary warehouse
wrapped in whorehouse curtains —
& the music
a capella elephants
jostling to be first back up the Alps
echoed like brays & slaps off each
soft cheek of the Virgin

4

in Rome we did what students do
make a racket & wish they were in Paris
(except the ones in Paris
who yearn for New York)
we stepped around the famous sites
ten years since John Keats died
arranged excursions to the local wines
planned longer trips to Venice & Milan
Florence   Naples   Palermo
Rome & the Academy left me cold
except for the shadows of the Colosseum
& the resonances of St. Peter's
it struck a chord in me forever
& I would step into serenity
as I left the heat of the city
for the cool beauty of elsewhere
I'd unpack some Byron
squat in an accommodating confessional
& read through spacious marble silence
the daft & burning passions
of our wine-dark wine-soaked hearts
until the dying of the light

5

the best days in Italy
were those spent walking
away from myself
along the lanes & tracks
that led from the city
across the plains of Lazio
towards the hill country
moving up into Abruzzo
in an old straw hat
& my pottering shirt
I'd grab a gun or guitar
& follow my unmissable nose
my head & tongue were heavy
with Virgil & key change
the ecology of orchestration
I stirred myself to tears
singing & composing
in the footsteps of the bard
I wept for Turnus & Lavinia
& I sang glittering armour
into being in the corners of my eyes
those walks were the only
perfect compositions of my life
the significant tremor of reed
gut & skin tuned to weather

6

I listen to bits of that
tinny pimp Rossini
with my knuckles
tuned to my teeth

I would rather have rusty skewers
hammered into my hips
than listen to one of his operas

Beethoven tends to come up
through the bowels like a
good suppository

I find I have to swallow
with consideration for timing
when listening to Mozart

the better the work
the more of my body is in my ear

originality in art
tends to be the juxtaposition
of several incompatible
anachronisms

7

each track & wood was
overshadowed by the Apennines
a monastery bell from the next valley
someone shouting behind a hut
a raucous bird coughing in a dead bush
just enough variety & dissonance
to help you recognise the planet
the music of the Abruzzi
is played with enormous verve
& self-confidence with each player
in tune irrespective of the others
& playing with impeccable timing
unlike one's colleagues
the bagpipes will make you forget
your future they just go in one ear
& stay there

8

don't forget to get ripped off
on a day trip from Naples
you can go anywhere
I went to Nisida
they emptied my wallet
treated me to a dinner so big
I could have sat in it
& lifted my feet off the floor
they felt guilty afterwards
& scurried around with much
furtive shouting before
presenting me with a keepsake
the biggest onion in the world
no I have not

9

it's always worth
popping into churches
& other sites
of uneasy need
& ambition
the music of yearning
of affiliation
self-satisfaction
or stomach-clenching
loneliness
you can watch
expressions postures
reflections & arches
& hear the loss
echoing through our rooms
the bigger the building
the greater the emptiness
underlined by every
art under the sun

Part 6

1

a young woman in white lay dead
in diagonal evening light
that sloped down through
the towering space of the Duomo
Santa Maria del Fiore
the young bride had died at noon
the priest hurried through the business
the body was trundled to a chapel of rest
for a final night above ground
in the vertiginous candlelight
the professionals mumbled
that which is mumbled
& slopped as much wet wax
about as they decently could
to be harvested immediately
by raggamuffins & then reused
at the expense of the next
family to be mugged by grief & loss
I stood in moving shadows
at the entrance to the resting place
& was invited in by a local
with his hand held out
I followed him in to the
otherwise deserted space
where he lifted her head
with its black hair & sad smile
& intolerable beauty: *È bella*
he grinned while letting her head
thump back down on the table

2

the echo of the thud
seemed absolute profanity
I froze like a statue of brutality
then melted & knelt
with her dead hand against my mouth
my guide still grinning
my heart imagined a young husband
suddenly appearing & misunderstanding
this gothic tableau
perhaps he would have deserved it
where was he how could he be elsewhere
& I dreamt goodbye to her
in Italian
forgive the strange intimacy
these stranger's tears on the pale
hand of death that can't take love
or my religion the arc of art
I left for another world

3

in Milan I went to the opera
but the whole audience was eating
drinking chatting picking each other up
playing cards & facing the wrong way
so I couldn't hear a note of Donizetti
music for the Italians seems to be
yet another kind of olive oil
something nice to drizzle on your
elevenses or whatever else is due
to be licked or inserted
in the next half hour
a tickle on the cymbal
a grope on the cello
a pounding in the background
on the big bass drum
it's all too voluptuous
& Italian for we French

4

all roads lead away from Rome
one way or another & I went home
a good six months early
I moved into Harriet's old flat
only to find she'd been back
& was still in Paris
as I prepared for my concert
she was back on the Paris stage in Shakespeare
that was no longer this month's flavour
slowly sucked downwards by debt
her spirits fell then so did she
she suffered a double fracture
& married me

5

one benefit concert featured
both Liszt & Chopin yet still
the cave of debt stayed dark
she brought her list of creditors
& I my anger
& the gristly business
of concert planning & self-promotion
we were ground together like
black & white pepper
I conducted & felt
a yawning chasm behind
which echoed nothing
but my pulse knocking

6

the micro-politics of the petty minded
almost showed the road to ruin
but you tunnel forwards like a mole
till one night the hall explodes
with praise & light
& Paganini pumping your arm
insisting on a commission

a work for orchestra & viola
to be played by the master himself

7

I decided the viola
would be me walking
through Abruzzo
like the lines of Byron
treading on through
mists & frustration
hangover longing
mind diseased with
its own beauty &
jagged aspirations
& yearning to cast off
definitively   still
I began to call in
notes from all over
the memory of being
borne upon that landscape
I allowed them to settle
above the magnet of
my heart let these describe
the indescribable

8

Paganini already dying
gave me a year's pay for nothing
so I could compose
for seven months I lived in
Romeo & Juliet to give back
what I could to Shakespeare
Paganini & Harriet
I hear it now
the introduction & adagio
Queen Mab
the haunted voice of Friar Laurence
'tis an ill cook that cannot
lick his own finger
if much of what you've made or done
doesn't move you deeply
it may be time to change your life

9

Spontini once told me
after hearing my Requiem
you know you are wrong
to moan about Rome
without Michaelangelo's
Last Judgement
you never could have
imagined your Requiem
actually the picture
disappointed me
I saw all the torments &
paraphernalia of hell
but nothing that could
help me see
humanity assembled
for one final bow

Part 7

1

heavily trembling on the thrumming tightrope
the art is lit & seemingly still
a twitch away from farce
on the edge of the credible
prone to misinterpretation
the memory is still in my throat
of the Funeral & Triumphal Symphony
to mark ten years
since the 1830 Revolution

the remains of those who died
over the Three Days
would be moved
to the new monument
in the Place de la Bastille
we'd crane our necks to look at Liberty
with wings outstretched
at the top of the column
moving with the souls of the
dead to heaven

2

I asked as many as I could
to the final rehearsal
I knew nothing
would be audible
on the day itself
in the windy vastness
of the Place de la Bastille
where the great crowd stood
as scraps of music flapped
about their heads
& disappeared
or the march to the square

but the music played
along the Boulevard Poissonnière
sang with great clarity

the band augmented
by great trees
that are no longer there

3

I wish you could have been with me
in Germany
it is so not-Paris
the musicians turn up early
the people love music as music
not as just another
symphony as handbag
fashion accessory
I loved Prague deeply
Liszt became breathtakingly
drunk & at two in the morning
was dead set on a duel
with some local drinker
his noon concert approached
he moved gingerly from bed
at 11.35 towards the piano
& played like a god

4

I wrote *Faust* swaying
on trains & boats
rattling along on a stage-coach
by gaslight in a shop one night
lost in Budapest
before dawn in Prague
& in every corner of Paris
I staked all I had on
two performances
at the Opéra-Comique
& no-one came
go to Russia
I am deeply moved
when I remember
how many people
helped me
pay my debts

5

I left Paris in deep snow
on Valentine's Day 1847
& for a fortnight
rocked hissing through snow
to St. Petersburg
ocassionally smiling at
the prophecy of Balzac
the night before I left
you'll return
a wealthy man
Balzac couldn't look
out of a window
without seeing earnings

6

once past the Russian frontier
the very air was torture
I was dragged swaying through
deep frozen ruts that kicked
my teeth around my head
in a frozen box on runners
battered travel-sick
frost-bitten to the
icy edge of death
in a day-nightmare I saw
soldiers crossing this terrain
without shoes or supplies
dead men walking
towards another freezing night
what does it cost to die

7

when I saw crows
fall on the horses' droppings
for food & warmth
I wondered why they stayed
instead of flying south
one hour into thawing out
my head in a hotel room
an invitation came to a
glittering short-term future
while back in France
men & women did
everything that men & women do
some die fast   some die slow

8

after six months of disgusting
suffering I lost my sister Nanci
she died of breast cancer
my sister Adèle stayed with her
& almost died herself
from the tearing pain of watching
I grind my teeth at the cruelty
of her prolonged incurable
Godless torture when a simple
anaesthetic could have
swallowed her pain for good
she died in early May
my wife died with less pain
a few came to the funeral
a quarter of a century earlier
when she was one of the stars of Paris
the city would have ground to a halt
to ease her to the grave

9

millions of details of scintillating
satisfactions & successes
mostly in Germany
add up to nothing in my cupboard
I smell failure even in the mirror
as you go downhill the world does too
the evidence is overwhelming
as I stumble through the outskirts
of town even when sat in the centre
I know my name & art will not survive

Part 8

1

I can't stop shaking
the laudanum makes me
thick & insensitive
& doesn't even take away the pain
she brought Shakespeare to Paris
Juliet Ophelia Desdemona
she opened up another world
in the mind of France
I walk through
the childhood of Christ
where I write my own words
& place them with my own notes
& none of it is mine

2

my first love
came back to haunt me
Estelle of the vine & hair
the white house on the hill
the little pink boots
there were times when I woke up
in the middle of the night
with a tune in my head
that pleaded to be kept
written down & teased out into life
I turned over & gritted my teeth
with tears mourning the ending

3

I will not speak about how
my love of Shakespeare was grafted on
my longer-standing love of Virgil
the most glorious episodes
of the Aeneid reawoken as a five-act
drama set to my mind's best music
I can't do more than cough it up
& spit in a pot
all I have left
on a planet past its sell-by date
is my son at the other end of the world
sailing towards some blade or grapeshot
carrying me with him from the
wreck of Paris & the wreck of life

4

Estelle has allowed me to
write from time to time
I have even visited
when my health permits
she knows that I am
twelve years old & she knows
better than I
that she is nearly seventy
I think of her every hour
I am always writing
the next letter
she knows better than I
that we will hardly ever meet again

5

my first & second wives
have both been dug up
& translated to a new edition
a grander monument
I saw everything
under the sun
& become smaller daily
my skull has shrunk
around my eyes
my son died
in Havana
of yellow fever
he was thirty-two
it was a day in June
it was just a day
& then there was another

6

I burnt the documents
cuttings letters
Royal commendations
attached to a past life
I visited Estelle
for the last time
in September
when winter came
I swallowed my future
for fuel & flared into
a final one-way flight
I took my soul to Russia
conducting concerts
in Moscow & St. Petersburg
Gluck Beethoven
Beethoven Beethoven
Beethoven Berlioz
running on empty

7

& then ignominious farewells
to the Mediterranean
I moved through my own estuaries
stumbling on the rocks
clattering face-first into stone
mistaking every bank & shoal
I heard noises in the air
malicious parodies of
outstanding lyrics
driven out of my head
the hills above Nice
felt like blasted heath
each of my vines
had died inside

8

Estelle is still alive
I want to erase time
walk with her up the coast path
to the hill overlooking the sea
there will be a white house
there will be vines & a flute
then orange groves
she will be eighteen
wearing little pink boots
I will be composing like a Trojan
& the rehearsals
at the finest opera house
in the world
are going well
I repeat myself often
just as the sea repeats itself
with every wave

9

my thoughts repeat themselves
the same thought passes through me
like a wave too early in spring
when the chill is not refreshing
but aches like a sick tooth or ear
I sent Estelle the words
I had written for *The Trojans*
& I asked her to read the page
marked with dead leaves
collected from the garden
of the white house
where she lived
when we were young

REALITY STREET titles in print

Poetry series

Kelvin Corcoran: *Lyric Lyric* (1993)
Maggie O'Sullivan: *In the House of the Shaman* (1993)
Allen Fisher: *Dispossession and Cure* (1994)
Fanny Howe: *O'Clock* (1995)
Maggie O'Sullivan (ed.): *Out of Everywhere* (1996)
Cris Cheek/Sianed Jones: *Songs From Navigation* (1997)
Lisa Robertson: *Debbie: An Epic* (1997)
Maurice Scully: *Steps* (1997)
Denise Riley: *Selected Poems* (2000)
Lisa Robertson: *The Weather* (2001)
Robert Sheppard: *The Lores* (2003)
Lawrence Upton *Wire Sculptures* (2003)
Ken Edwards: *eight + six* (2003)
David Miller: *Spiritual Letters (I-II)* (2004)
Redell Olsen: *Secure Portable Space* (2004)
Peter Riley: *Excavations* (2004)
Allen Fisher: *Place* (2005)
Tony Baker: *In Transit* (2005)
Jeff Hilson: *stretchers* (2006)
Maurice Scully: *Sonata* (2006)
Maggie O'Sullivan: *Body of Work* (2006)
Sarah Riggs: *chain of minuscule decisions in the form of a feeling* (2007)
Carol Watts: *Wrack* (2007)
Jeff Hilson (ed.): *The Reality Street Book of Sonnets* (2008)
Peter Jaeger: *Rapid Eye Movement* (2009)
Wendy Mulford: *The Land Between* (2009)
Allan K Horwitz/Ken Edwards (ed.): *Botsotso* (2009)
Bill Griffiths: *Collected Earlier Poems* (2010)
Fanny Howe: *Emergence* (2010)
Jim Goar: *Seoul Bus Poems* (2010)
James Davies: *Plants* (2011)
Carol Watts: *Occasionals* (2011)
Paul Brown: *A Cabin in the Mountains* (2012)
Maggie O'Sullivan: *Waterfalls* (2012)
Andrea Brady: *Cut from the Rushes* (2013)

Narrative series

Ken Edwards: *Futures* (1998, reprinted 2010)
John Hall: *Apricot Pages* (2005)
David Miller: *The Dorothy and Benno Stories* (2005)
Douglas Oliver: *Whisper 'Louise'* (2005)
Ken Edwards: *Nostalgia for Unknown Cities* (2007)
Paul Griffiths: *let me tell you* (2008)
John Gilmore: *Head of a Man* (2011)
Richard Makin: *Dwelling* (2011)
Leopold Haas: *The Raft* (2011)
Johan de Wit: *Gero Nimo* (2011)
David Miller (ed.): *The Alchemist's Mind* (2012)
Sean Pemberton: *White* (2012)
Ken Edwards: *Down With Beauty* (2013)
Philip Terry: *tapestry* (2013)

For updates on titles in print, a listing of out-of-print titles, and to order Reality Street books, please go to www.realitystreet.co.uk. For any other enquiries, email info@realitystreet.co.uk or write to the address on the reverse of the title page.

REALITY STREET depends for its continuing existence on the Reality Street Supporters scheme. For details of how to become a Reality Street Supporter, or to be put on the mailing list for news of forthcoming publications, write to the address on the reverse of the title page, or email **info@realitystreet.co.uk**

Visit our website at: **www.realitystreet.co.uk/supporter-scheme.php**

Reality Street Supporters who have sponsored this book:

Alan Baker
Andrew Brewerton
Peter Brown
Paul Buck
Clive Bush
Mark Callan
John Cayley
Adrian Clarke
Dane Cobain
Mary Coghill
Kelvin Corcoran
Ian Davidson
David Dowker
Carrie Etter
Gareth Farmer
Allen Fisher/Spanner
Penny Florence
Hilary Fraser
Sarah Gall
John Goodby
Paul Griffiths
Chris Gutkind
Charles Hadfield
Catherine Hales
John Hall
Alan Halsey
Robert Hampson
Tania Hershman
Gad Hollander
Simon Howard
Fanny Howe
Romana Huk

Elizabeth James
Keith Jebb
L Kiew
Peter Larkin
Sang-Yeon Lee/Jim Goar
Richard Leigh
Tony Lopez
Chris Lord
Richard Makin
Michael Mann
Lisa Mansell
Peter Manson
Ian Mcewen
Ian McMillan
Geraldine Monk
Pete & Lyn
Dennis Phillips
Tom Quale
Josh Robinson
Lou Rowan
Will Rowe
Jason Skeet
Valerie & Geoffrey Soar
Alan Teder
Philip Terry
Paul Vangelisti
Juha Virtanen
Susan Wheeler
John Wilkinson
Johan de Wit
Anonymous: 5

www.ingramcontent.com/pod-product-compliance
Lightning Source LLC
La Vergne TN
LVHW041156080426
835511LV00006B/621